180 BUSINESS HACKS

180

BUSINESS
HACKS

Little Changes, Big Difference

Roel de Graaf

JOHN
MURRAY
BUSINESS

First published in Dutch by Boom Uitgevers Amsterdam in 2021.

English edition published by John Murray Business in 2025

An imprint of John Murray Press

1

Dutch edition design by Justus Bottenheft.

English edition design by Janette Revill.

Images licensed from Alamy.com

A CIP catalogue record for this title is available from the British Library

Hardback ISBN 9781399811347

ebook ISBN 9781399811354

Typeset in Avenir LT Std 9/12 by Integra Software Services Pvt. Ltd., Pondicherry, India

Printed and bound in Great Britain by Clays Ltd, Elcograf S.p.A.

John Murray Press policy is to use papers that are natural, renewable and recyclable products and made from wood grown in sustainable forests. The logging and manufacturing processes are expected to conform to the environmental regulations of the country of origin.

John Murray Press   John Murray Business
Carmelite House   123 S. Broad St., Ste 2750
50 Victoria Embankment   Philadelphia, PA 19109
London EC4Y 0DZ

The authorised representative in the EEA is Hachette Ireland, 8 Castlecourt Centre, Castleknock Road, Castleknock, Dublin 15, D15 YF6A, Ireland

John Murray Press, part of Hodder & Stoughton Limited

An Hachette UK company

CONTENTS

INTRODUCTION

Conventional thinking will get you conventional results. Sometimes you just need a bit of inspiration. Something to help you get away from the daily grind and see things differently. This book contains hacks to give you a different perspective at work. They're all easy to read, proven to work and might even put a smile on your face. Often the most impactful ideas are small, and, like tiny cracks, they eventually produce something bigger.

The hacks are organized into nine themed chapters so that you can find them quickly if you need them. You might even enjoy simply flipping through and opening a page at random to see how the hack applies to your work.

Thanks to Alice de Graaf and Karena Freeman for their valuable feedback. A special thanks to Iain Campbell and Meaghan Lim for for their tireless and meticulous efforts in reviewing and editing this work and the selection of these 180 hacks from the larger database available, and to Amanda Jones for very capably managing production. Janette Revill also did a great job in the design of the English edition. And of course a big thank you to Margriet, who is always there to provide me support and challenge.

If you have a business hack you would like to share, please let me know. Maybe you will find it in the next edition.

Have fun reading and applying the hacks!

Roel de Graaf

PART 1

INNOVATION

THE MARTINI PRINCIPLE

Anytime, Anyplace, Anywhere

Martini once had an advertisement with the slogan 'Anytime, Anyplace, Anywhere.' I call this **The Martini Principle** and it's a great model for innovation. Any product, service or process that does not meet the Martini Principle can (and should) be improved. Can I purchase your product or service at any time, at any location, in any manner? If not, you need to act fast. Or others will.

THE AMAZON WAY

Follow **the Amazon Way**. When developing a new product, service or process, first draft the press release. After the press release, write the Q&A. Once you've finished that and the stakeholders are enthusiastic, only then start the development process. Working backwards greatly increases your chances of success. If it works for Amazon, it'll work for you.

Brian Dumaine – *Bezonomics: Leren en winnen van Amazon* (original Dutch title)

OUTSIDER'S PERSPECTIVE

Sometimes it helps to look at your organization from an **outsider's perspective**. Question the obvious. Does everything we're doing make sense? What do we take for granted that prevents us from innovating? There are all kinds of ways to do this but the best is to become a client of your own organization and experience the product or service yourself. When was the last time you looked at your organization from the outside in?

YOUR NIGHTMARE COMPETITOR

A nice exercise for planning and strategizing is to create your own nightmare. What might a competitor do to really challenge your organization? By doing this exercise with your team, an interesting scenario emerges. It reveals the weaknesses of your organization. It pinpoints areas where you need to improve and become better. What does your **nightmare competitor** look like?

ELIMINATE
SIMPLIFY
STANDARDIZE
AUTOMATE

How do you reduce complexity? By applying Edward de Bono's **ESSA** sequence: eliminate, simplify, standardize and automate. But remember the right sequence! You'll be surprised how often elimination is the solution!

Edward de Bono – *Simplicity*

Edward de Bono was a physician and renowned commentator on creative thinking. He originated the term lateral thinking, and wrote many influential books including *Six Thinking Hats*.

CHANGE THE RULES

Innovating is **changing the rules** of the game. Air travel is a great example. Historically, it was based on sea travel: the pilot's uniform resembles a ship captain's uniform, we have (air)ports, boarding, first and second class, the 'hub-and-spoke' model. Then came companies like EasyJet who changed the rules of the game by looking at the way US coach companies worked: direct flights instead of hub-and-spoke, variable fares, different check-in methods. What could you glean from other industries? What 'rules' could you break in your industry?

REVERSE MENTORING

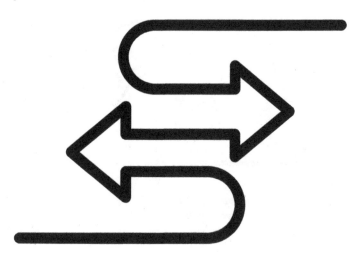

Junior staff always know best which of your products, processes and ways of working could be improved or simplified. Additionally, if they are digital natives, they are more aware of the possibilities that technology can bring.

Could you implement **reverse mentoring** in your organization? Consider regularly assigning senior executives to junior employees for an hour and have the junior employee show them how they can work more efficiently.

MIRROR THINKING

You may have noticed that a lot of elevators have **mirrors** nearby or inside. This isn't a coincidence. Mirrors are there so you have something to do while you wait for the doors to open.

You could spend lots of time and effort making the elevators run faster, with algorithms to determine the best floor position for them to be on standby when waiting for someone to press a button. Or, just shorten the perception of waiting time for your users. Could you use this kind of thinking for your next challenge?

HACKATHON

A **hackathon** is a great method for energizing your organization and generating possible solutions to a problem in a short timeframe.

It is an event where people come together to dive into specific problems. The hackathon will often start with a presentation about the event, then participants, in teams of about 2-5 based on individual interests and skills, suggest ideas and solutions. At the end of the hackathon each group presents their results.

ONE BRIGHT IDEA

A manager once sent me on a training course. I said that I was already familiar with what was being discussed. Their response never left me: 'If you come back with just one bright idea, it will have been worth it.' **One bright idea** and the investment will have paid off. When you head back to the office after your next training session, what idea will you bring back with you to action?

 **DO LUNCH**

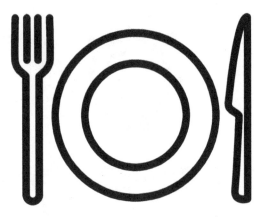

Do lunch with an outsider – someone beyond your team or organization. Bring them an issue you're grappling with and see what their approach is. If it doesn't fit, no harm done. If it does, you've discovered a whole new source of ideas. Lunch with an outsider broadens your perspective. And let's face it, you're going to be having lunch anyway, so what have you got to lose?

FREE INSIGHT

In *The McKinsey Way*, an old McKinsey associate explains how the company operates. One suggestion is getting **free insight** from your competitors, which is a great way to accelerate innovation in your own organization. There is a wealth of information available – for free – in publications, in presentations and online. People love to talk about how good they are and luckily that information is easily accessible. You could even search for information about your own organization. You'll be surprised at what is available.

Ethan M. Rasiel – *The McKinsey Way*

REAL TIME IS TOO LATE

There's a great concept from *Marketing in the Digital Age*: **real time is too late**. If you are responsive, you are too late.

Take a look at how Apple knows the lifespan of a phone and approaches customers proactively with an offer for a new device around when their old phone's lifespan comes to an end. What data do you have on your customers and potential customers, and how can you use that to proactively improve your services?

John O'Connor – *Marketing in the Digital Age*

UNBUNDLING

To understand how markets and organizations develop, it's good to take a look at airlines again. Originally, they performed all their own operations: buying and maintaining aircrafts, employing pilots, catering and so on. Nowadays, everything is done through specialized businesses. Specialization is everywhere if you **unbundle** your operations. What activities does your organization do in-house that a specialist could do more effectively?

THE WATCH MODEL

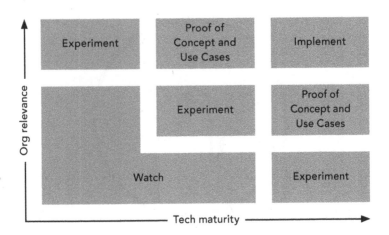

This is a helpful model for deciding whether it's time to step into a technology or stand back and **watch**. If you want to be a pioneer you don't need this model, but for everyone else, plot the technology in this diagram and then decide how to proceed accordingly. This avoids wasting time and resources.

EARLY SUPPLIER INVOLVEMENT

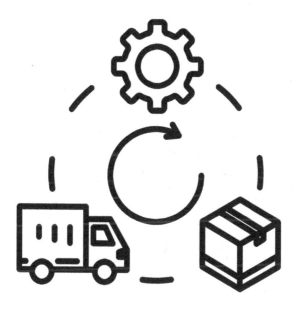

Early Supplier Involvement is a concept in manufacturing which recommends involving your suppliers early in the development of a new product to accelerate and improve the process. It can be very beneficial. At one organization, a Purchasing Director requested suppliers submit proposals to reduce costs. It was a great success. Give it a try.

LEARN FROM YOUR RIVALS

You can learn a lot from your **rivals** even if you don't get along with them. Who are your main competitors and what are they doing right? Put yourself in their shoes. What would you do if you were in their position? Why are they doing what they do? You can always learn. Get used to seeing your opponents differently.

DO THE RIGHT THINGS

When the Americans began space travel, they spent a million US Dollars on developing a stylus that could write in any circumstances. What did the Soviets do? They used a lead pencil. The key is to stress the importance of doing the things that matter. Do things right. **Do the right things**.

UPSET PEOPLE

Imagine coming up with an innovation that could potentially undermine your organization's entire business. That's exactly what happened to Steven Sasson, inventor of the digital camera at Kodak. In an interview with MT/Sprout, he shared a very important lesson about innovation: 'Realize that you have to change, even if you don't see the point in doing so. Even if your customers don't ask for it. You have to create scenarios about what could possibly happen.' He said that you'll know you're doing a good job as an innovator if you manage to **upset people**. How many people have you upset today?

ADD-ONS

For many companies, the product they are known for is no longer
the main source of revenue. The real gains are made in the **add-ons**.
Basic car models are almost never bought. At gas stations, the shop
is like a supermarket. And think about booking a flight. The luggage
costs almost as much as the seat! Is your organization leveraging the
add-ons?

PART 2

STRATEGY

THE NAPKIN TEST

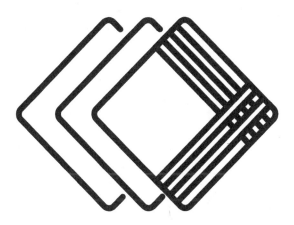

Strategy documents can often be long and unwieldy, which completely defeats the point. Large documents are often not read, let alone used. Even a one-page strategy can be too much (especially as they're often in a tiny font to fit on the page!) In *The Back of the Napkin*, Dan Roam says that a strategy should fit on a **napkin** or it's too long. If you can do that, you've got the right strategy.

Dan Roam – *The Back of the Napkin*

TELL PEOPLE WHY

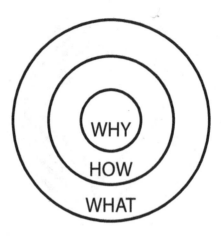

Don't tell people what to do. Don't tell people how to do it. Tell them **why** it is important to do. If you can articulate the why, their actions will follow.

Simon Sinek – *Start with Why*

TOUGH CHOICES

Are you brave enough to make tough choices? Do you have what it takes to say no to good ideas?

Steve Jobs did. In an annual planning session, all sorts of ideas were proposed and eventually a list of the top 10 was made. Quite an accomplishment, most would say. Not Steve Jobs. He told his management to only focus on three of them. Real focus is a **tough choice** to make, but it allows you to be successful at what matters most.

FIRST LOOK BACK

Are you familiar with those fancy strategy documents describing how everything is going to change? Magnificent visions for the future overflowing with ambition. To ensure a level of realism, it is a good exercise to take a moment to reflect on the past. What has been achieved in a given period to date? With no radical changes (like injecting much more money, more people, better quality materials), this is what you can expect to accomplish in the upcoming time frame too. With this in mind, do you need to **first look back** and have a reality check?

ONE-HOUR STRATEGY

You might know how to tell people about your strategy but getting it down on paper is often a challenge. A proven way to resolve this is to find someone you work well with and involve them in the process. Take it in turns, spending just one hour each at a time. First you write down the key elements of your strategy in your hour, then share it with your partner who does the same for the next 60 minutes. And so on until it's done. **One hour** provides focus and breaks down a challenging task into manageable chunks. You will be surprised with what you can achieve.

FUTURE-BACK THINKING

Studies show that strategic plans rarely materialize. So how can you ensure that yours is a success? One idea is to start with the ultimate objective and then work backwards. So instead of the classic 'this is where we are and this is what we want to achieve', try flipping the model on its head. Think from the **future** outcome and **think** your way **back**, down to what you need to do right here, right now.

Tanya Prive – 'Why 67 Percent of Strategic Plans Fail'

SCENARIO PLANNING

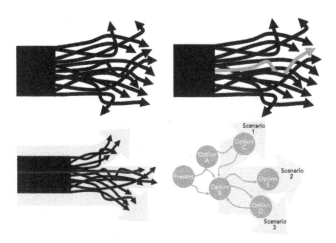

Every organization should be doing **scenario planning**. But scenario planning isn't about choosing the best possible path to go down. Scenarios provide insight into what the main trends are and allow you to prepare for the most likely outcomes.

What you get if it's done well is informed options that leave you with no regrets no matter what scenario happens. It gives you room to manoeuvre decisively. So, what are your options?

10 10 10

Minutes.   Months.   Years.

In **10-10-10,** Suzy Welch introduced a transformative new approach to decision making. The process is clear, straightforward and transparent: when you're facing a dilemma, all it takes are three questions: What are the consequences of my decision in 10 minutes? In 10 months? And in 10 years? This will give you the right information to make a well-informed decision. Exploring the impact of your decision in multiple time frames surfaces your unconscious agendas, fears, needs and desires – and ultimately helps you identify and live according to your goals and values.

Suzy Welch – *10-10-10*

STRATEGIC PLAN IN A DAY

It's perfectly possible to write a **strategic plan in a day**. If you have a good table of contents and start collecting what's already available, you can easily create version 0.1. And that's usually the hardest part. Expanding it further and incorporating all the additional ideas from everybody involved is way more straightforward. Give it a try. See if you can get to version 0.1 in 1 day. It's easier than you think.

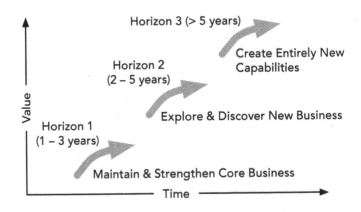

3 HORIZONS

Horizon 3 (> 5 years)

Create Entirely New Capabilities

Horizon 2 (2 – 5 years)

Explore & Discover New Business

Horizon 1 (1 – 3 years)

Maintain & Strengthen Core Business

Value

Time

You might hear strategy practitioners say something like, 'We are now focusing on Horizon 2'. In that case they're referring to a model that McKinsey introduced to identify the focal point of the strategy session. Horizon 1 focuses on the here and now, Horizon 2 on the near future and within existing contexts. Horizon 3 takes a long-term view to ensure the continuity of the business. A great example of an organization with an adequate focus on Horizon 3? Philips: from light bulbs and electronics to healthcare. As an organization, are you paying enough attention to each of the **Horizons 1, 2 and 3**?

Julie de la Kethulle de Ryhove – 'What is the 3 horizons model & how can you use it?'

FLIP-OVER MODEL

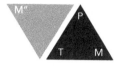

The '**Flip-over model**' is genius in its simplicity. When applied to the Product – Market – Technology paradigm, it says that if you plan to start creating something new as an organization, you have the best chance of success if you 'flip' over one axis. So, with an existing product and an existing technology to a new market, or with existing technology in an existing market with a new product. You always have two anchoring points. Which axis will you flip over?

THE HYPE CYCLE

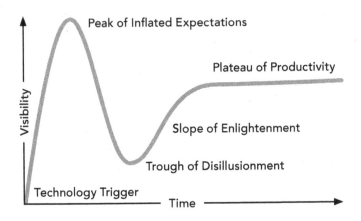

The Gartner **Hype Cycle** is a great tool for revealing the evolution of any technology. Innovation is paradoxical; while people overestimate the short-term consequences of technological innovation, they underestimate the long-term impacts. Have this in the back of your mind when it comes to new developments. Don't get in too early, but be aware that, after the phase of disappointment, you have to start thinking about how it will impact your organization and be there when it takes off.

REDRAW THE MAP

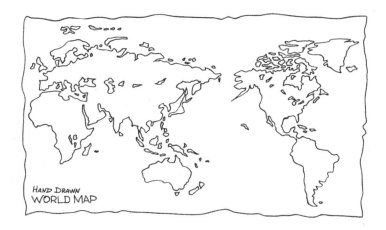

HAND DRAWN
WORLD MAP

Depending on where you live, it might seem strange to see China **drawn in the centre of the world map** with Europe and the USA pushed to the outer rim.

But this is what the world looks like from an Asian perspective and it's a perspective we as Europeans and Americans will have to get used to. Many people agree that the past 200 years of US dominance will come to an end with China and India rising to prominence again. As an organization, how are you preparing for this change?

SUSTAINABILITY GOALS

More and more organizations are aware that it's not all about making money these days. They are thinking long term and have incorporated **sustainability** into their strategy and vision. However, the translation of sustainability into practice is not always straightforward. Look up the United Nations' 17 Sustainable Development Goals.

Which of these 17 goals could your organization make a meaningful and valuable contribution towards?

CUSTOMERIZE

cus-to-mer-ize/'kɔstə,mī rəz/ **Verb** 1: We help our customers to better serve their customers. 2. To make a company more responsive to its customers and better be able to attract new ones **syn** *see customer, competitive edge, business critical priorities.*

In the early years of my career, I worked for Unisys whose vision was: 'We help our clients to serve their customers better.' In a word: **customerize**. This is a great mindset. Everything you do should be about your customers. And about your customers' customers. This mindset is beneficial for any organization and any team – no matter what industry you're in. Remember: Help your customers serve their customers better!

TOP LINE AND BOTTOM LINE

2.16

Top Line

  Bottom Line

All innovations and advancements by organizations are ultimately centred on two goals: increasing both the **top line** and the **bottom line**. In accounting, the top line refers to a company's revenues or gross sales. The bottom line refers to a company's net income after deducting costs. For top line improvement, it is about tapping into new revenue streams with new products and services and getting access to new markets and clients, or retaining and expanding existing customer bases. In order to optimize the bottom line, it is essential to reduce costs by improving operational excellence and to manage and control risks. When assessing proposals for improvement this is key: what is the impact on the top and/or the bottom line?

KNOW YOUR KPIs

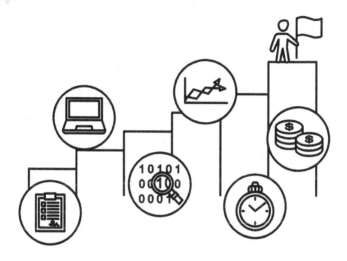

The big problem with dashboards and metrics in many organizations is that there are far too many Key Performance Indicators (KPIs) and not enough understanding of their meaning.

What does the dashboard in your organization look like? Does it clearly identify areas that are performing well or where corrective action is needed? Effective management with **a limited set of KPIs**: that's what dashboards, metrics and KPIs are all about.

INTERVIEW FROM THE FUTURE

This is a thought-provoking exercise for when you're starting a new strategy or a new project. Imagine being **interviewed by a reporter from the future**. How would you answer questions such as: 'What was the key to your success?', 'What made a difference?' and 'What could you have done better?' This exercise will give you a good view of what you want to achieve, what is important in approaching it and what the risks are. It's also a great team building exercise at the start of any project!

IT GOES WITHOUT SAYING

The best feedback you can get when you present something new in your business is: **'that goes without saying**!' If that is the response after showcasing your strategy, your vision or a proposed change in organizational design, then you know you're doing great. If it makes sense to your internal stakeholders, the implementation and execution will be much more straight-forward.

OPTIMISM

Sometimes it is good to hear a **positive voice** amid all the cultural pessimism that prevails. Since 2000, the European economy has grown by 20% while the use of raw materials has declined by 5%. Anyone growing up in the 1980s will recognize this. Your room was full of all kinds of devices that used up a large amount of raw materials. And what are our kids using now? A smartphone. More functions and better quality than all those appliances back then. That's progress!

Ralf Bodelier – 'Ontkoppeling. We doen méér met mínder'
(original Dutch title)

PART 3

STRUCTURE

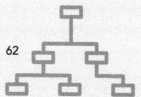

FIND YOUR 2IC

Do you have **a second-in-command (2IC)** on your team that you can entrust tactical and operational tasks to, freeing you up to focus on more strategic work? There is probably a talent up for the task, allowing them to gain experience and preparing them for the next step. And importantly, this also paves the way for you to take the next step. You have your successor ready. Who's your 2IC?

Thanks to Paul Hermans

FLIP THE ORG CHART

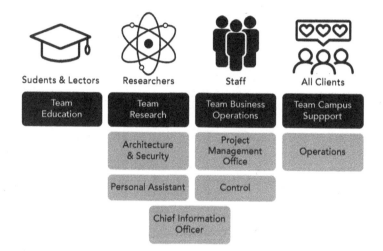

Next time you create an **organizational chart** (or 'org chart'), put your customers at the top and your frontline employees underneath. They are the ones having the day-to-day interactions with your customers. This way, staff, managers and directors get a position on the org chart in line with their role: supporting the employees. This makes for a refreshing way to look at your organizational structure. Plus, it ensures that your customer has a place in your org chart!

Inc.com – Flip your org chart upside down

CHAORDIC

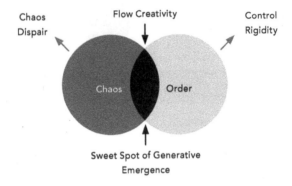

Chaos
Dispair

Flow Creativity

Control
Rigidity

Chaos

Order

Sweet Spot of Generative
Emergence

Chaordic is such a great word – Chaotic and Order! Dee Hock, the founder of VISA, discovered that the more rules he introduced, the less people thought about their actions, but if you don't have any rules at all, people don't know how to act. He discovered that rather than creating detailed how-to manuals, it is better to have clear principles that give people direction.

Dee Hock – *One from Many*

THE RHINELAND MODEL

3.04

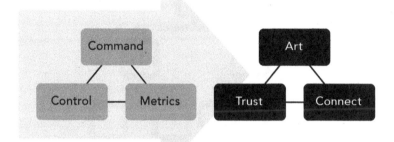

In recent decades we have been bombarded with American management thinking, but gradually we are witnessing a reversal. Shareholder value is no longer the only thing that matters. Employees are no longer 'resources'. The real value of an organization lies in the hands of empowered individuals who embrace self-management, teamwork and trust. The **Rhineland model** is helping organizations succeed by prioritizing cooperation, consensus, social justice and the interests of multiple stakeholders. Could this help your organization?

Peters, Brouwer, Janssen & Weggeman – *Rijnlands Organiseren* (original Dutch title)

TOP LEFT, BOTTOM RIGHT

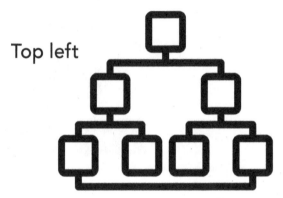

Top left

Bottom right

Warning! After reading this, you will never look at an organizational chart in the same way again. In many Western cultures, people tend to structure an organizational chart from **top left** to **bottom right** with the most important departments top left and the departments that will be in trouble in the next restructuring bottom right. Whenever I've pointed this out, the response has been: 'Yes, but I didn't consciously sketch it this way'. That is precisely why it is so true.

Unconsciously, we place the most important thing at the top left and the least important at the bottom right. So where is your department in the org chart?

Thanks to Paul Valens

TEMPORARY, NOT PERMANENT

Here's a curious phenomenon. If you organize temporary work in a permanent way, it becomes self-sustaining. Think of data quality staff. If you turn them into a formal department, they will continue to find work. It's a vicious cycle. So **don't organize temporary work in a permanent manner**. Organize temporary work in a temporary way, for example through specific projects.

CORPORATE MEMORY

Do organizations have a memory? Strangely enough, they do. A striking example was a consultancy assignment I once received. I got a call from a procurement officer asking if we wanted to review their project. We didn't know anyone involved in the project, and yet they turned to us because years ago we had done some similar work at the organization. We were part of the **corporate memory**.

When making decisions, should you be examining what's in the collective memory of your organization?

RACI TABLES

	Role 1	Role 2	Role 3	Role 4
Task 1	R	C	I	A
Task 2	I	I	R	A
Task 3	C	R	A	R
Task 4	A	R	I	
Task 5	R	A	C	I
Task 6	C	C	A + R	I

1 A
1 R

RACI tables are used in management to map roles and responsibilities with the letters of the acronym defining whether someone is Responsible, Accountable, Consulted or Informed about the corresponding task. RACI tables with multiple Rs & As in a row are a disaster waiting to happen. If multiple people are responsible, then ultimately no one is responsible. This is known as the Ringelmann Effect: 'I thought that's what the other person would do!' RACI tables should only ever have one R and one A per row to ensure that everyone's responsibilities are crystal clear. If this is impossible, try breaking down the activity. By getting one level more detailed, you prevent a lot of problems.

FIREFIGHTING

3.09

There's a tendency in organizations to put firefighters on a pedestal – the people who fix malfunctions and work late if there are problems. Fortunately, there's a growing appreciation for employees who prevent problems happening in the first place. People who have everything under control because they do things properly. Sometimes it takes a blazing fire to raise awareness among management and the board of the need for these silent workers. For example, cyberattacks that occasionally appear in the press. Then, they appreciate that **prevention is better than firefighting.**

YOUR BRAIN BUDDIES

Are you an original thinker? Or is your mind stuck in the world of ready-made opinions and solutions? Gaspersz calls this reproductive thinking: where we are numb and no longer generate spontaneous and original thoughts. He also has a great solution. You can prevent it from happening by surrounding yourself with people who are good at listening, questioning and inspiring one another. He calls it your **Brain Buddies** where people with different backgrounds get together periodically to exchange ideas. Who would be your Brain Buddies?

Gaspersz – *Anders denken nieuwe kansen* (original Dutch title)

NON-BILLABLE TIME

David Maister is the author of the standard guide for those in professional service firms like consultants or lawyers. One of his best quotes relates to **non-billable hours**: "your billable time is your income, your non-billable time is your future". This is the activity that defines the future. It could be developing new services and products, publishing new articles, optimizing operations or other such activities. What is your organization's approach to employee down time? Are you sufficiently maximizing the potential of these hours?

David H. Maister - *Managing the Professional Service Firm*

OPT-IN TEAMS

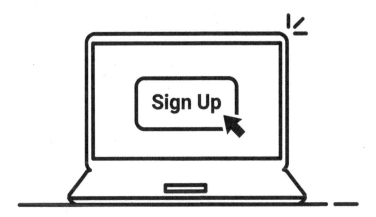

Instead of managers selecting team members, allow people to opt themselves in. It avoids mismatches where people aren't enthused by the project or the rest of the team. **Opting in** sends a message of agility and autonomy to the organization. It also allows teams to de-select members if they don't contribute. It will increase productivity and success. Employees within an organization naturally select its priorities: ask yourself "what is wrong?" with an initiative if nobody opts in.

THE TWO-PIZZAS RULE

In the early days of Amazon, Jeff Bezos set a simple rule: each internal team should be small enough to be sufficiently fed with only **two pizzas**. This measure accomplishes two objectives: efficiency and scalability.

The first is clear: a smaller team spends less time on internal communication and more on what needs to be done. But it's the latter that's really essential for a business like Amazon: adding new product lines also means needing to add new internal structures, new meetings, projects or processes.

YOUR COBOT BUDDY

Collaboration between robots and humans is becoming increasingly common so prepare to meet your new colleague: a Cobot or **Collaborative Robot**. Of course, robots have been working on the assembly line for years, but they are now more common in office spaces too. If you're working late, you might see a Cobot vacuuming while its human colleague cleans the desks. Or think about the Chatbots working alongside real people in call centres. Artificial Intelligence (AI) is the new assistant for the office worker. Are you ready for a Cobot buddy?

DICTOCRACY

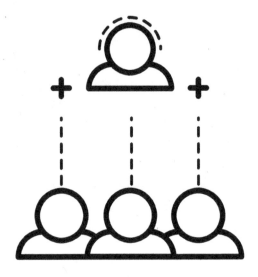

A decision is not the beginning of a dialogue, it's the end of it. Anyone can participate in the debate before a decision is made. All contributions are welcome. But ultimately someone has to make the call and arrive at a decision. And when that decision is made, everyone has to go for it and leadership has to stand behind it. Consultation and involvement ahead of the decision (**democracy**) and firm leadership to stick to decision once it has been made (**dictatorship**). Is the decision always respected as the end of the discussion in your organization?

Thanks to Lucien Zalbin

EMBRACE THE STORM

Psychologist Bruce Tuckman described how teams move through four stages: forming, storming, norming and performing. During the forming phase, everyone is trying to find their place as a team member. **Storming** is where expectations turn out to be different, miscommunication happens and tension builds. You should try to get to this phase as soon as possible as it will help the team get to the performing stage quicker. After this, expectations are realigned and new ways of working are agreed. Finally, you can hit the ground running and deliver results.

THE 25% TIPPING POINT

According to research by Damon Centola at the University of Pennsylvania: the **tipping point** for a change in society can be precisely identified as **25%**. If 25% of a population embraces a new notion, then the change will happen. As soon as someone joins the group of change-makers to bring that group up to 25%, then change suddenly happens. In this context, informal social networks play an important role. In your case, which 25% of employees will be your change agent?

Loeffelholz – 'The 25% Tipping Point'

YOUR SKILLS PASSPORT

3.18

According to Lizette van Neer-van Dingenen, it's time to ditch the traditional CV in favour of a **skills passport**. Sure, graduating is a milestone, but nowadays it's all about skills – and these require continuous maintenance as they become obsolete fast. She advises categorizing skills into three tabs: foundational skills, essential for every employee in your organization; role-specific skills, necessary to excel in particular positions; and future-oriented skills, areas where employees can, should or must develop to remain competitive for the future. What skills set you apart in the job market?

YOU GET WHAT YOU MEASURE

Key Performance Indicators (KPIs) are an effective control mechanism. A KPI is a **measurement** that shows how the organization delivers on selected factors. It is important that you carefully consider which aspects to measure as the indicators will quickly determine the behaviour within your organization. Yes, this is what you're aiming for, but there will also be unintended side-effects. Have you heard about the case of bank employees opening accounts for customers without notifying them? That was one of their measures of success, and what should have made a positive contribution actually turned out negative.

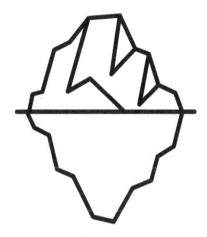

FOCUS ON INTERESTS

3.20

Principled negotiation, as described in *Getting to Yes*, encourages you to share and explore the **deeper interests** underlying your stated positions and to negotiate on the merits in order to reach the desired outcome quickly and to mutual benefit. It describes the four main elements of principled negotiation:

1. Separate the people from the problem.
2. Focus on interests, not positions.
3. Invent options for mutual gain.
4. Insist on using objective criteria.

Have you tried this negotiation strategy?

Fisher, Uri & Patton – *Getting to Yes*

PART 4

MANAGEMENT

DO NOT DISTURB

facilitate   coach   disturb

60%   35%   5%

Managing is 60% facilitation, 35% encouragement and 5% **disruption**. Ensuring that employees are able to perform their tasks is at the very core of effective management. Try not to **disturb** or interfere, just pave the way and make sure there are no obstacles. Be available when things aren't running smoothly. But know that sometimes you have to shake things up, so be ready to be disruptive if the business gets stuck or too cozy or stuffy.

TAKE A WALK

Who would have thought that one of the best ways to manage is to simply get up and **walk around**? It's so simple but hardly anyone does it. When I suggested it to a management team, one of the managers replied: 'But when will I have time to do my regular work?' They had not quite grasped the concept of being a manager yet. This is the real work: to be there for your team, to be there for your people. Even in times where we do more and more work remotely, this is still great advice. Your team will appreciate you being available for them and not just sitting in meetings all day. Plus, you will gain some knowledge from it as well!

HIRE BETTER PEOPLE

In the words of Howard Wilkinson, English footballer and coach, if you **hire people who are smarter than you,** maybe you are showing that you are a little bit smarter than them. Fill your team with people who are better than you. Surround yourself with superstars above your level. You'll get better results, if you dare.

BE LAZY

Bill Gates famously said that he would always find a lazy person to do a difficult job because you could rely on them to find the easiest way to do it. It may be one of the Seven Deadly Sins, but **lazy people**, especially managers, are often the most productive and smartest. Why? Simple:

- They work smart.
- They use resources wisely.
- They know how to prioritize.
- They don't multitask.
- And most important of all, they don't interfere with other people's work.

Martin Waaijer – *De luie manager* (original Dutch title)

NO SURPRISES

Here's a simple rule to agree on with your team: **no surprises**. You never want to get into a situation where you're confronted with something your boss knows about before you. It happens all too often. Good news travels fast; but how quickly can you rely on being told about the bad news?

Agree on this with your team and do the same for yourself: always inform your boss in advance. Never leave the door open for surprises!

OVERLY RESPONSIBLE

Don't be **overly responsible** for what is happening in your organization, your department or your team. This has two risks:

- Firstly, your people will step back if they know you are taking care of it. Worse, they'll increasingly drop things on you and before you know it, you'll be handling everything.
- Secondly, if you're constantly mopping up after other people, you are not doing what you were hired for in the first place: coming up with the vision, delivering the strategy and managing stakeholders.

Everyone is responsible for their own problems, so don't try and take on everything yourself.

GIVE SOMEONE BUSY MORE WORK

4.07

If someone is very **busy**, find **more work** for them to do. When you give a busy person more work to do, it teaches the art of delegation. They will have to hand over tasks to someone else so that they can focus on what really matters. It is the best way to teach someone how to organize for effectiveness versus organizing for their own efficiency.

THE FEEDBACK FALLACY

Received management wisdom is that there's nothing better for a manager to do than praise or criticize the work of their reports – generously sharing the benefits of their years of experience. But it turns out that **feedback** – telling people what we think of their performance and how they should do it better – **is not actually that useful** after all. On the one hand, research shows that we're not actually very good at rating other people's performance. In fact, the way you rate people says as much about you as it says about them. And on the other hand, neuroscience now shows us that all criticism achieves is to activate the brain's fight or flight response. Criticism *inhibits* learning. The most powerful role a manager can play is to spot people doing good things. How are you giving feedback?

Buckingham and Goodall – 'The Feedback Fallacy'

THE NEXT STEP

When taking the next step in your career, don't simply focus on the job itself. Every job is a stepping stone to another. Treat each job as an **option** for the next job and the job after that. So, when you take your next step, carefully reflect on where you want to be in the next step beyond that. Then choose and make your move.

KNOWLEDGE, ABILITY, DRIVE

Knowledge   Ability   Drive

Selecting your team is not always easy. What do you look for when you are recruiting? An easy principle is: '**knowledge, ability and drive**'.

Knowledge is about whether they have knowledge of the topic. Ability is about skills and how they interact with others.

When it comes to drive, it's all about the attitude. Are they committed? Will they go the extra mile? Drive is without a doubt the most important. When things don't feel right in the drive department, there is only one decision: don't bring them into your team!

YOU CAN EITHER MEET OR WORK

Peter Drucker once said that you can either **meet or work** but you can't do both at the same time. Think about that when you attend your next meeting. Could you achieve the same result without it? You could be doing yourself and the other participants a big favour.

Peter F. Drucker - *The Effective Executive*

MEETING HACKS

ELIMINATE
- ❏ Don't schedule meetings
- ❏ Don't attend meetings
- ❏ Don't agree to meetings

STREAMLINE
- ❏ Have an agenda
- ❏ Have a facilitator
- ❏ Have an out

These 9 meeting hacks can help you get back hours each week

REDUCE
- ❏ Reduce frequency
- ❏ Reduce length
- ❏ Reduce drive-by meetings

When run properly, meetings provide an excellent structure for getting work done, making decisions and moving projects forward. Wrongly delivered meetings, however, keep you from focusing on your key priorities and are a waste of time. If you find yourself struggling to do the work, take a closer look at the time you spend in meetings and rebalance this with your real priorities. Elizabeth Grace Saunders' nine hacks will help to **reduce the time you spend in these meetings**.

Elizabeth Grace Saunders – 'These 9 Meeting Hacks'

LEAD BY EXAMPLE

People don't do what you say, they do what you do. Whether you're at the top – leading your organization, in the middle – managing a team or at the bottom, set an example for everyone around you. From the big decisions right down to the basics of showing up on time, **lead by example**.

UNDERSTAND, THEN OUTSOURCE

If things are not running well, outsourcing is not the solution. When something is outsourced, you still have to manage it. If that didn't work well in-house, do you think you'll get a different result with someone else in charge? What you don't **understand** you can't manage, and what you can't manage you can't **outsource**.

DE-REGULATE

Years ago, in the Dutch city Drachten, they removed all the traffic lights, signs and markings from a roundabout. As a result, traffic flow improved and the number of accidents reduced significantly. The traffic was regulated by de-regulating it. People had to be more aware and think more when driving in those areas. This is a wonderful example of how you can think about rules in a different way. **De-regulating** made things work better. What rules are getting in the way in your organization?

Berthold Gunster – *Huh?*

GET YOUR PRIORITIES RIGHT

In Dutch, the last part of 'priority' is pronounced the same as the word for 'time'. The message is: there is always time. If someone doesn't have time to do a certain activity, they are in fact saying that they have other priorities, that other matters are more important. So have a think about what really matters most.

BE CONSCIOUS OF YOUR WEAK POINTS

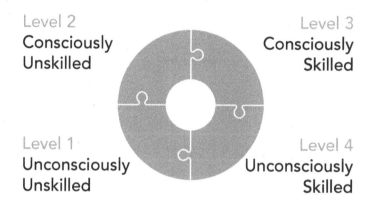

I once knew a consultant who was an incredible problem solver. There was no one better at analyzing and getting to the bottom of a problem. The only chink in his armour was that, as someone with dyslexia, he found spelling people's names challenging. As a client, there is nothing more annoying than receiving a report where your name is spelled incorrectly. Our consultant was well-aware of this and always had the names checked by a colleague before he submitted his report.

Are your team members conscious of their weak points?

20 : 70 : 10

Jack Welch, the man who once made General Electric the most valuable company in the world, had a simple rule: **20-70-10**.

It's called the vitality curve. Of your employees, 20% are top performers, 70% are what you need to keep the organization running and the bottom 10% have to go.

Recruit new talent, new enthusiasm and more diversity. Keep improving!

THE GOLDEN RULES OF APPRAISALS

There are two simple **rules for the end-of-year appraisal**. Rule 1: No news. If you have to mention something about performance from the past year, it shouldn't come as a surprise to the employee. Rule 2: if something is worth including in the appraisal, it should be backed up by at least two specific examples, whether positive or negative.

Give two concrete examples and no vague arguments, a single incident is not enough. Use these two simple rules as guidance – your employees will appreciate it.

SEGMENTERS AND INTEGRATORS

The sociologist Van der Lippe distinguishes between **segmenters** and **integrators**. Segmenters prefer to separate work and private life. They might even prefer not to work from home at all, for the sake of their own productivity. Integrators can easily visit the gym during working hours but can also take a phone call for work during private time. They let it all blend into one. It's good to know what type of person you are, as a partner and a colleague, so you can account for your own, and other people's, needs.

PART 5

ANALYSIS

SPOT THE COMPLICATION

Situation

Implication

Complication

Resolution

A good consultancy analysis follows this structure:
- Situation – what's going on?
- Implication – what are the consequences, what is the impact?
- Resolution – what is the solution?

There is however another important step: **Complication** – why hasn't it been fixed in the past? Only once you answer this question is it safe to start working on the solution. If a problem has existed for some time, it's safe to assume that several attempts to solve it have already been made. Why have these attempts failed?

SQUEAK AND SQUAT SIGNALS

In train railways, a squat is a surface defect on the rail caused by metal fatigue. Do you have an eye for the '**squeak and squat signals**' in your organization? Maybe you didn't get the progress report on time. Maybe there are things missing in reports, or the project lead is ill when there is an important meeting. These are the signals that something is probably not right. We often respond to the symptom and not to what is happening below the surface. These kinds of signals are important because they show that there is probably more going on and quite often tell more than you'll find in the reports themselves.

Thanks to Eric Kemperman

FOLLOW THE MONEY

At the business school INSEAD, I once had a professor who told me that if you want to know an organization's strategy, just ask them what they're spending their money on. If you **follow the money**, you'll soon discover what's important to the organization and what they prioritize.

THE 80/20 PRINCIPLE

20% 80%

If you're not familiar with the **Pareto principle** or Richard Koch's brilliant books on **80/20**, you should change that fast. It states that 80% of your results come from just 20% of your time. Getting to a 100% result – increasing the result by a mere 20% – would take a disproportionate amount of time so why would you bother when 80% is enough? All the extra effort is superfluous. 20% of the time, 80% of the result. Think of what you could achieve.

Richard Koch – *The 80/20 Principle*

THE 400% FORMULA

20%	80%
20%	80%
20%	80%
20%	80%
20%	80%
100%	**400%**

We've already discovered how using the 80/20 principle can get you 80% of the results in 20% of the time but there's an additional nuance here; in addition to an 80% result being good enough, the productivity gains of working with 80/20 are staggering. You can accomplish four times as much in the same time. **400%** performance instead of 100%. It's mind-blowing what you can achieve if you focus on getting to 80% and not worrying about the last 20%. Think about how this could transform your efforts, your team and your organization.

Richard Koch – *The 80/20 Principle*

THE THEORY OF CONSTRAINTS

You'll find the **Theory of Constraints** in *The Goal* by Eli Goldratt, a great book about optimizing your operations. Basically, what he said is that an organization is only as good as its weakest link and you need to find the weakest link in your chain of production. If you can identify it and make it twice as efficient, the output of your organization will increase dramatically. So where in your process is the weakest link?

Eli Goldratt – *The Goal*

THE 4-HOUR TIME SAVER

A manager once helpfully instructed me: 'Before you start creating something yourself, spend **four hours** checking whether anyone else has already created anything similar that you could reuse.' What a great piece of advice. Don't jump into anything, first explore. These four hours might save you and your team a lot of time and effort.

INITIAL HICCUPS

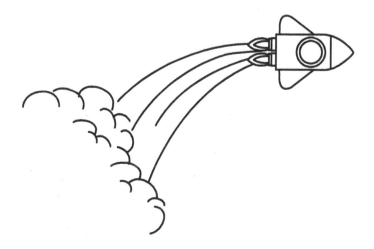

When a project kicks off and encounters a rough start, it's often attributed to **initial hiccups** – nothing too concerning, just part of the process. But according to Bent Flyvberg, a Danish expert in megaprojects, these initial hiccups actually signal deeper issues: either the plan itself isn't sound, or the team might not be sufficiently equipped to handle the task. By intervening decisively at the early stages – either by halting progress or reshuffling the team – it's possible to avert numerous issues that might plague the entire project. Would you take decisive action if things didn't start off well?

FIND THE DESIRE PATH

A **desire path** is the shortest or most easily navigated route between a starting point and a destination.

Desire paths emerge as shortcuts where official pathways take a circuitous route. Rather than convincing people to use the official route in your organization, could you find a way to adapt to the desire paths that emerge?

WORD CLOUD ANALYSIS

Here's a great use for **word clouds**. If you want to review a strategy, plan or document, to see if it is really addressing the right things, put the text in a word cloud generator tool. A strategy document should be about the customers. If that doesn't come through in the word cloud, ask yourself if the document is really focused on the right things.

OCKHAM'S RAZOR

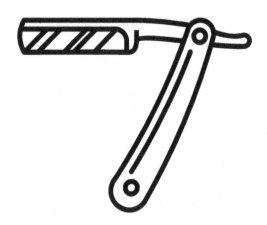

Ockham was a 14th century monk who, amongst other things, researched logic. He was the inspiration for the sharp protagonist in Umberto Eco's novel *The Name of the Rose*. One of his finest legacies is **Ockham's Razor**, which states that if there are several possible solutions or explanations to a problem, then the most straightforward is most likely the right one. Keep Ockham's Razor in mind whenever you're struggling with a challenge.

96 ANALYSIS

3X1 BRAINSTORMING

The 3x1 method is a nice way to start **brainstorming**. Give all participants a stack of Post-Its and ask them to write down ideas for one minute without conferring (one idea per Post-It). Then ask the participants to pass the Post-Its to their neighbour and give them another minute to continue or build on the ideas in front of them. Repeat this one last time, then work together to rank and select. You will be surprised how many ideas can be generated in just three minutes!

BECOMING FUTURE-PROOF

One of the things you learn in requirements analysis is that you shouldn't just solve today's problem, you should also see how you can **anticipate future demands**. Is everything you're doing future-proof, or is your team only solving what's right in front of them?

THE PURPLE CROCODILE

In the Netherlands, the term **purple crocodile** is a metaphor for bureaucracy, originating from a 2005 TV advertisement by the Dutch insurance company OHRA promoting their lack of red tape. It symbolizes everything to do with strict procedures, customer-unfriendly processes and unreachable organizations. Are there any areas in your organization that would qualify for a Purple Crocodile Award? If so, take action!

THE PROBLEM WITH EFFICIENCY

Too much focus on efficiency in an organization can be the **fastest way to the wrong goal**. Of course, it's important to have good espresso in the kitchen but really, it's a place for informal conversations. A coffee maker on every desk would be efficient, but completely miss the point. And of course, you can skip a business trip and run the meeting on Zoom but it won't show your client you value them enough to invest in a day of travelling. When chasing efficiencies, be careful not to chase out common sense too.

LAST IN, FIRST OUT

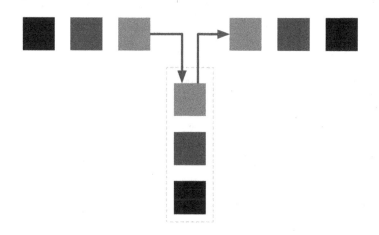

Backlogs. Sooner or later, we're all going to have to deal with them. I've noticed that often, we start with the oldest project in the log.

This seems logical because 'they have been on the list for so long', but it is very often far better to operate on a **Last In, First Out** basis. Priority 1 is to avoid any new delays. Priority 2 is to keep the customers who haven't been waiting long happy. The final priority is cleaning up the old items as quickly as possible and with all the necessary care for the customer.

BATNA

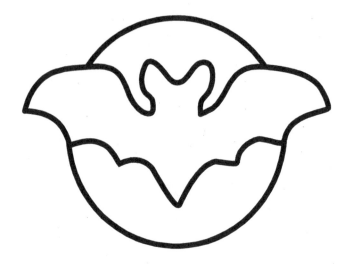

BATNA stands for **Best Alternative To No Agreement**. What is your alternative option when you're negotiating?

Anton Philips, CEO of – you might have guessed it – the Philips company, was a grand master at it. His core philosophy was: don't depend on anyone. During negotiations he ensured that there was an alternative option at all times. In this way he could, without fear of failure, keep on making additional demands or aborting negotiations at the last minute. He became known as a very sharp negotiator for good reason. What is your BATNA next time you go into a negotiation?

FACTS ARE FRIENDLY

Facts are friendly. Facts underpin the direction of the resolution. Facts compensate for feelings. Facts ensure that you are being taken seriously. If you want to succeed in an organization, if you want to change things, make sure you have all the facts at hand. In fact, make sure you have a better understanding of the facts than everyone else in the room. Know the facts.

DON'T FORGET FEELINGS

Feelings are a fact, according to Peter Block in *Flawless Consulting*. The previous hack pointed out that facts can compensate for feelings, but emotions have to be considered as well. It is not all just logic and reasoning. How something is perceived has a great influence. So, it is important to pay attention to emotions when analyzing and making changes. Are you fully aware of the vibes and emotions that exist in relation to your business?

Peter Block – *Flawless Consulting*

BROWN JACKETS VS BLUE JACKETS

Organizations are made up of **brown jacket and blue jacket** personalities. Blue jackets are the ambitious employees, keen on getting ahead in their career. Brown jackets are the people who do the work and who really know what's going on. When things aren't running smoothly, the brown jackets are more useful than the blue jackets in finding the solution. With the lack of dress codes that require jackets now, it's not as obvious as it was, but it's still possible to figure out who the brown jackets are when you need them.

Thanks to Paul Valens

PART 6

SIMPLICITY

YOUR LIGHTBULB MOMENT

The **invention of the light bulb** didn't come from simply perfecting the candle. It came from recognizing the task at hand and then taking a step back to explore entirely **new solutions**. You could invest significant time and effort in making a candle burn longer and brighter, but it would always just be a candle, not a light bulb. Before diving into a problem, strip it back to basics and ask yourself: 'What am I really looking for?'

Margarita Tokareva – 'The Dark Side of Process Improvement'

FIND THE SIMPLE SOLUTION

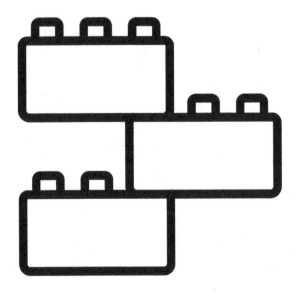

Engineer Leidy Klotz had a revelation while playing Lego with his two-and-a-half- year-old son. When a piece was missing to level a scaffold, Klotz went looking for it, while his son ingeniously removed a cube from the longer leg to solve the issue. This prompted Klotz's research at the University of Virginia, where he discovered a fascinating tendency: our natural inclination is to complicate rather than **simplify**. When confronted with a problem, we often opt for solutions that involve adding elements rather than eliminating existing ones. The reason behind this remains unclear but it happens repeatedly in many situations. Maybe it's time to start simplifying things!

Simone van Neerven – 'We blijven investeren in complexer, maar de oplossing zit in simpeler' (original Dutch title)

SPECIALISTS HATE SIMPLICITY

The easiest way to establish superiority is to introduce complexity. Complexity requires specialists and experts to explain it which gives them an elevated position. If something is simple and easy to understand, it removes their role, so don't expect **specialists** to take the initiative in **simplifying** anything. It is not in their interests. The initiative to simplify needs to come from somewhere else. How could you make things simpler every day?

Edward de Bono – *Simplify*

KILL YOUR DARLINGS

Anyone trying to create a simple product, service, experience or piece of communication must be ruthless when it comes to editing, refining or, to use a harsher word, killing. Hollywood filmmakers use the phrase '**killing your darlings**' when referring to a scriptwriter's painful task of deleting something they love – whether it's a colourful scene, a quirky character, a clever line – that doesn't advance the story. Similarly, when simplifying at work, there's no substitute for being a ruthless killer.

Alan Siegel & Irene Etzkorn – *Simple: Conquering the Crisis of Complexity*

FRICTION HUNTERS

Every organization should appoint a '**friction hunter**', according to Steven van Belleghem. Friction hunters are employees who identify, prioritize and resolve friction in the customers' experience. A great example is Amazon Go where you never have to stand in line at the checkout. It is imperative to make the customer experience as enjoyable and efficient as possible. Time is a scarce resource, so make sure your customers' time is well spent. Could this work in your organization?

Steven van Belleghem – 'De nieuwe marketeer is een friction hunter' (original Dutch title)

6.06 LEARN FROM THE SMALL

In management literature, the focus tends to revolve around well-established companies, seen as the models to learn from, but smaller organizations are often more creative. For example, small businesses have to be just as technically advanced as their larger counterparts, but limited resources mean that they often seek smarter, more innovative solutions on their own. Necessity is the mother of invention. **What could a small company teach you** about practical, agile business practice?

THE EFFORTLESS EXPERIENCE

If you want to have loyal customers, you have to **minimize their effort at every touchpoint**. Keep reducing the energy and time they spend to get what they want from you. Look at every aspect of the customer journey, every touchpoint a customer has with your organization, whether face-to-face, on the phone or online. Make it easy. And not only when they want to buy something, but also when they want to stop using a service. Loyalty is something to cultivate over the long term.

Dixon, Toman and Delisi – *The Effortless Experience*

SPEED EQUALS SIMPLICITY

No one likes the frustration of waiting. All of us try to find ways to speed things up. When an interaction happens quickly, we put the efficiency down to the perceived simplicity of experience. Achieving notable efficiencies in speed are exemplified by overnight delivery services like FedEx and even the ordering process for a McDonald's hamburger. When you have to wait, life seems unnecessarily complex. **Savings in time feel like simplicity** and we are gratefully loyal when it happens.

John Maeda – *The Laws of Simplicity*

MAXIMUM CLARITY

Whether you're an online retailer or your product is a project-management enterprise solution, **maintaining and maximizing clarity** in the user interface is key to user success and satisfaction. Clarity allows your users to understand what you're trying to help them achieve. If your design has too much unnecessary information, users will have trouble navigating your site. Call attention to only the core aspects of the page you want them to focus their attention on within the first few seconds of browsing.

Euphemia Wong – *Simplicity in Design: 4 Ways to Achieve Simplicity in Your Designs*

AVOID AVERAGE

6.10

With your head in the freezer and your feet in the fireplace, your temperature is about average, but I'm afraid you're not doing well. Watch out for the use of averages. **Averages can be quite an inaccurate measurement** if, for example, there are large outliers on either side. Those outliers can give you a great deal of information. Take, for example, a measurement of customer satisfaction. The outliers in the positive direction are your promoters. The outliers in the negative direction can give you valuable information about how things can be improved. You learn nothing from the average.

Thanks to Lucien Zalbin

FAILURE FRIDAY

Giny Boer, CEO of C&A, introduced Failure Friday to the organization. It's a concept originating in the agile/IT sector where Fridays are used to look for bugs in the systems. She applies it slightly differently: leaders make themselves vulnerable on **Failure Friday**. As a leader, you discuss a mistake and consider the lessons learned and what needs to be done to prevent it happening in the future. Would you dare to embrace this concept? It might be a simple way to learn and grow.

THE PERFECTION PARADOX

6.12

What's wrong with striving for perfection? Quite a lot according to Bohré-Den Harder. **Perfectionism** seems great, but it can also get in the way and often has a social component: the urge to do things very well, consciously or unconsciously, to get approval from the outside. In fact, a perfectionist raises the bar so high that the perfect result is unattainable. It is never good enough. And then the disadvantages emerge: perfectionism leads to procrastination, stress and burnout. Do you recognize the perfectionist in your team? Do they know the 80/20 principle?

Marjon Bohré-den Harder – *De Perfectieparadox*
(original Dutch title)

ONE PICASSO A DAY

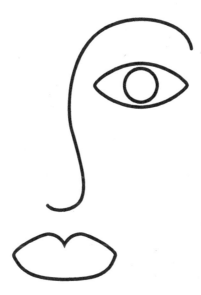

Limit yourself to one Picasso a day. That's the advice from Karin Swiers at MTSprout, distilled from Adam Bryant's book *The Leap to Leader*. Don't get distracted by too many priorities. Decide in the morning what your one masterpiece that day is going to be and, in the evening, look back and admire it. Bask in your success. You can only do one thing well at a time. If you've succeeded at one thing, you'll sleep a whole lot better.

Karin Swiers – 'Met deze 4 tips raak je niet overweldigd in je nieuwe leiderschapsrol' (original Dutch title)

DON'T CHASE TWO HARES

There's an old French saying: **'If you hunt two hares you'll catch none'**. It applies to work too. If you do two things at once, you will get two, at best, mediocre results. When you concentrate on one thing, you can do it really well. To do something to the best of your ability demands your full attention and dedication. If you start chasing two hares . . . you know what happens.

DON'T PUT IT OFF

You'd expect the main purpose of a meeting to be to make a decision, so why is it that decisions so often get rolled over to another meeting? **Don't put it off**, decide now. You can stop this by introducing a simple rule: if someone proposes postponing a decision to the next meeting for a second time, then that meeting is cancelled. This creates a problem-solving culture, rather than one where problems get passed on. It sends a signal that the group is meant to tackle difficult topics.

SIMPLY AUTOMATE

Legend has it that flying a modern plane requires little or no intelligence; pilots are highly trained and educated but aren't expected to use their knowledge and skills other than in control mode. Whether or not that is the case, much of the work we see as intelligent is already routine from a technological perspective and can be replaced by intelligent systems. And with the rise of Artificial Intelligence (AI), knowledge work is also on its way to becoming routine from technological reality. What work in your organization could **simply be automated**?

Tissen, Andriessen, Deprez & Lekanne – *Value-based Knowledge Management*

SIMPLE KNOW-HOW

A machine broke down in the factory, bringing production to a halt. A mechanic was called in, who spent a few minutes talking to the machine operator and listening to the sounds coming from the machine. He walked over to the machine and hit it at a point where three pipes merged into one. The machine immediately sprung into life. The manager received a $500 invoice from the mechanic. He asked why it cost so much and received the itemized bill the next day: 'One hammer blow: $0.50. **Knowing** where to hit: $499.50. Total $500.'

START A 'GOT DONE' LIST

Always take time to acknowledge and enjoy your successes, however big or small. Focus less on your 'To-Do' List and more on your **'Got-Done' List**. Look back at what you have accomplished at the end of the day. Have a small party for yourself. It feels good to bask in what you've achieved. It's a simple and effective way to build confidence and momentum. Can you put this on your 'Got-Done' List for today?

Stacy Kim – 'Forget To-Do Lists. You Really Need a 'Got Done' List'

THE RULE OF ONE

Idea
Reader
Promise
Action

In marketing there's a golden rule: **The Rule of One.** One powerful argument is more effective than many semi-argumentative ones. The more arguments you use, the less effective each one will be. The Rule of One is one of the foundational principles of copywriting. It states that whatever copy you write should focus on one big idea, one reader, one promise and one call to action. What is the one argument you'll use in your next pitch to win over your audience?

Thanks to Christ Coolen

THE ART OF DOING NOTHING

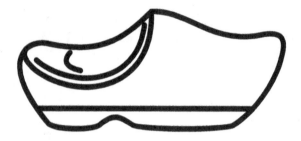

'Niksen' is a Dutch word meaning to make a conscious choice to sit back, let go and **do nothing** at all. No scrolling on your phone, no yoga or Zen meditation. Niksen at home: Find a comfy chair and sit. That's it. Niksen at work: Stare at your computer or take in the view. Niksen is not about working smarter. It is about taking a break from all the busyness and giving yourself sincere, heartfelt permission to do nothing. And when you are doing nothing, or 'niks' in Dutch, the best ideas pop into your head.

Olga Mecking – *Niksen: Embracing the Dutch Art of Doing Nothing*

PART 7

CHANGE

WHAT WENT WELL?

Boris Grundl was once a very promising professional tennis player who broke his neck and was left 90% paralyzed after a dive off some rocks went wrong. How he picked his life up again is a very impressive story. At a German congress I was at, he spoke and shared a simple rule: spend 5 minutes every day thinking about **what has gone well**. It's so much better to focus on what you can do than what you can't do.

Apply this within your organization, within your management team and even at home, with your children. Concentrate on what's going well. It creates a good vibe. It develops self-confidence.

DON'T TELL PEOPLE WHAT TO DO

No-one likes being told how to do things. You've just got started and some smart ass comes along and tells you to do it differently. The truth is, people do want to change, they just don't want to be changed. So set goals, give direction, but don't bore them with the 'how'. Let them figure it out for themselves.

WHAT'S IN IT FOR ME?

When change happens, our first thought is often **'what's in it for me'** – how it will affect us and if we will benefit. This is a perfectly healthy example of self-interest. Knowing that people put their own interests first gives you something to use to your advantage – something that is well-understood in sales. How could you use this insight with your own team?

MAP THE ORGANIZATION

This is a great exercise for bringing organizational issues out into the open. **Draw a map** featuring all of the departments.

Which one is on an island? Where are the mountains of problems? Where are the cities of stakeholders? The outcome is always interesting and once you're ready, start exploring the organization through the map.

THE LAW OF CONSERVATION OF ENERGY

The law of **conservation of energy** states that the energy you put into something is the same as the energy that comes out. Do you think you can solve something without putting much time into it? Keep in mind that it will take up more of your time later on. And vice versa, if you've prepared it very well, it will be easier down the line. Even better: if you present something with a lot of enthusiasm, that enthusiasm will definitely come back to you. Energy is contagious.

CHANGE FACTORS

Vision	Skills	Incentives	Resources	Action plan	=	Change
	Skills	Incentives	Resources	Action plan	=	Confusion
Vision		Incentives	Resources	Action plan	=	Anxiety
Vision	Skills		Resources	Action plan	=	Resistance
Vision	Skills	Incentives		Action plan	=	Frustration
Vision	Skills	Incentives	Resources		=	Treadmill

Here's a practical checklist for when you meet resistance to change from your employees or teams: **vision, skills, incentives, resources, action plan = change**. If any of the elements before the equals sign is missing, then the change won't work and it will backfire. Have you made sure you've covered all the elements for your next change?

WHO'S TAKING NOTES?

Do you want to make sure that everyone in your team pays full attention during meetings? Then **rotate the person who takes the notes** and don't announce until the end who the notetaker is. You can be certain that everyone will stay focused in future!

STAY IN BED

Do you ever feel like you have your best ideas in the shower? Well, Scott Barry Kaufman - a cognitive scientist and co-author of 'Wired to Create' – conducted a study showing that 72% of people have creative ideas in the shower.

Other places include walking, exercising and lying in bed. Kaufman 'stresses the importance of relaxing for creative thinking' because creativity comes free when you're relaxing. So, if you're struggling with a problem: just **stay in bed**.

> Kaufman – '72% of people get their best ideas in the shower'

AN OUTCOME EVERY WEEK

As a partner in a consulting firm, my team and I had an agreement that we would achieve an (intermediate) outcome every week during an assignment for a client. **Every week we would deliver a tangible result**. This gave us a clear focus. What (intermediate) outcome could you or your team achieve to surprise your customers or organization in the coming period?

THE ADAPTABILITY QUOTIENT

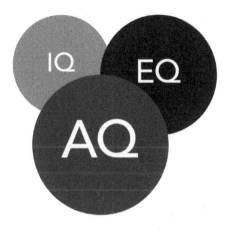

The way we work, live and relate to one another is fundamentally shifting. Extraordinary technological advances in automation, artificial intelligence, disruptive innovation and globalization have resulted in an unprecedented rate of change. The **Adaptability Quotient** (AQ) is the ability to determine what's relevant, forget obsolete knowledge, overcome challenges and adjust to change in real time. Those with a high AQ demonstrate the following behaviours: open-mindedness, an active desire to view situations from others' perspectives and the prioritization of developing new skills. How is your AQ?

Callum Hughson – 'Adaptability Quotient'

THE FACES OF RESISTANCE

- ✓ Give Me More Detail
- ✓ Flood You With Detail
- ✓ No Time
- ✓ Impracticality
- ✓ I'm Not Surprised
- ✓ Attack
- ✓ Confusion

- ✓ Silence
- ✓ Intellectualizing
- ✓ Moralizing
- ✓ Compliance
- ✓ Methodology
- ✓ Flight into Health
- ✓ Pressing for Solutions

One of the highlights of *Flawless Consulting* is Peter Block's description of **the faces and forms of resistance** you might experience when presenting your advice on a change. It's a kind of bingo card for consultants featuring: silence, give me more detail, no time, attack, confusion, intellectualizing, moralizing and many more. Which faces of resistance have you encountered in steering committees, from employees or colleagues?

Peter Block – *Flawless Consulting*

WIN – RESULTS

Win   Result

A lot of research has been done on how best to convince someone to buy something. The standard reference book for salespeople is *Sales Strategy* which states that if you want to sell something to someone, two things are important: how your product or service contributes to the organization (result) and how it contributes to their personal goals (win). Think in terms of '**win – results**'. Apply this to your stakeholders when you want to accomplish something in your organization. The result for the organization is obviously important, but you will surely receive a 'go' if you are also able to play to their personal win.

Miller & Heiman – *Sales Strategy*

THE ART OF MANAGEMENT

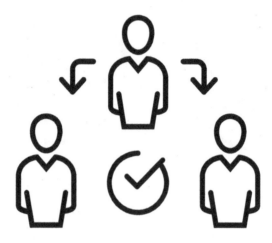

Are you familiar with those managers who strive to be the top-dog, always in the lead? It's a trap people fall into when they're put in charge. **The real art of managing** is not managing at all. The real secret of management is **facilitating, enabling** and **empowering** people to be successful on their own. A great manager provides the right resources and the right support and most importantly, gives people credit when they are successful. A true change manager ensures these conditions are in place, they relish the success of others and as a result, they are highly successful themselves. Are you that kind of manager?

THE THIRD WAY

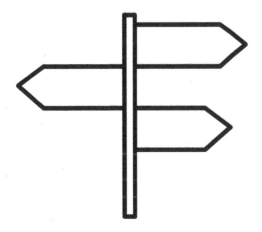

When presented with a decision, many people anchor on the two most obvious opposing options. This type of either/or approach unnecessarily imposes limits on your thinking, causing you to miss opportunities to combine ideas or find a third outside the mould of the original two. To push people out of either/or thinking, ask them for a **third option**. When forced to think beyond their existing options, they not only generate another option, but break the constraints of the mental model they've been using.

Matt Plummer, Founder, Zarvana

COUNTERING RESISTANCE

You probably recognize the person in your organization who turns resistance on to the max when a change is imminent. No argument will convince them. So how do you **counter resistance** and get someone like that on board with the change? Make them responsible for its successful implementation. When it works out, a permanent brakeman becomes the driver: the poacher becomes the gamekeeper.

UNWRITTEN RULES

Every culture has its own customs and traditions and when we deal with foreign countries, we know that we have to take that into account. But every organization has its own culture too – **unwritten rules** such as formal and informal manners or a way of making decisions. Take for example the new senior manager who could not understand why his excellent proposal was not approved by the Board of Directors, unaware that all members of the Executive Board had to be consulted first when such a proposal was discussed. Look out for the unwritten rules in your organization so that you know how to navigate them.

UNDER PROMISE AND OVER DELIVER

What could be smarter than **under promising and over delivering**? All too often the opposite happens.

Wonderful plans are made promising all kinds of things and then afterwards you have to go back and apologize for the disappointment. You've set yourself up to fail with your own overly ambitious plans. Why not flip things around? Be slightly less ambitious in your plans, but all the more ambitious in the execution. Doesn't that sound good?

FIND YOUR MR. WOLF

Remember **Mr. Winston Wolf** from the movie *Pulp Fiction*? He solved problems. Do you have a Mr. Wolf around in case anything needs fixing? Someone you can call into action if you've hit a crisis, or the wheels start falling off. A fixer. Someone who turns things around and solves them for you. Everyone needs a Mr. Wolf, so who's yours?

RESISTANCE IS GOOD

Resistance to change isn't necessarily a bad thing. Resistance is first and foremost a signal that change has been initiated and that something is happening. Perhaps employees are right when they openly express their doubts about the change. Perhaps they are identifying issues that have not yet been taken into account. They are often 'closer to reality' and therefore have insight that management may not yet possess. So, listen carefully to what people in opposition have to say. It can only prove beneficial.

A FOOL WITH A TOOL

'A fool with a tool is still a fool', as the saying goes. When an organization tries to resolve its problems with yet another new tool, this regularly crosses my mind. 'Once we have implemented the new tool, things will run more efficiently', is what they usually say. But many issues in organizations can't be solved with a tool. When the people who have to work with the tool don't have the right knowledge or skills, another tool won't fix the issue. People are still the ones that make a difference in organizations, technology is just a supporting instrument.

PART 8

IMPACT

KEEP IT SKETCHY

Don't present a plan as a done deal. That works against it being accepted. If you show a customer a plan that has been worked out in detail, they will probably reject it. There's nothing more they can do. It's not their job, it's yours. **Show them a sketch**. Explain it, talk them through it, let them use their imagination.

Get them involved. You can also apply this when you present a plan to your board, your colleagues or your employees. Present a concept. The best thing you can do is leave space for them to come up with proposals to make it even better.

Paul Arden – *It's not how good you are, it's how good you want to be*

So now what?

A good presentation has a clear structure. 'So now what?' is an easy easy-to-use mnemonic for ensuring that your presentations are easily understood. It contains three simple questions that need to be answered in every presentation. **What? So What? Now What?** You don't need a series of PowerPoint slides to achieve that.

INFLUENCE

1. Reciprocity

2. Scarcity

3. Authority

4. Consistency

5. Liking

6. Consensus

In his classic book *Influence*, Robert Cialdini describes six ways you can encourage people to act: reciprocity, scarcity, authority, consistency, liking, consensus. You see these used on all kinds of websites these days. For example, if you want to book a hotel, you might see: 'only 1 room available' (scarcity) or 'an 8.4 rating from XXX' (authority). What sources of **influence** could help you achieve your target?

Robert B. Cialdini – *Influence*

YOU CAN'T COACH A GHOST

When you're coaching, you can't give advice to someone who's not in the room. In the conversation, focus on the person sitting at the table. Don't respond to statements like 'the others agree with me' or 'a lot of people do it as well' or anything that brings people who are not present into the conversation. Focus on the participants. It's about what they actually have to say. Don't be tempted to engage in a conversation with 'the others'. **You cannot coach a ghost**.

THE HARDEST QUESTION

When you're giving a presentation or running a meeting, be prepared for the most difficult question that can be asked. And plan in advance what the best answer to that question would be. If you're already prepared for the **hardest question** ahead of time, the session itself will be a piece of cake.

TELLING STORIES

Storytelling is hot. As a leader you can use **storytelling** to sketch a bright future. It's important to speak imaginatively and let people visualize the future. If they can visualize it, it's life. Take them from a dull text to colourful imagery. Give it a try. The more imaginative the more memorable.

René Boonstra – *Storytelling*

SMART BREVITY

If you've ever worked on a document with someone else, you'll recognize how easy it is to get into a quarrel over a specific word or a part of the text. The solution is in many cases very simple: remove it. You'll be surprised how often **smart brevity** turns out to be the best solution. It's a bit like the 'Elsschot ordeal', where Flemish writer Willem Elsschot introduced an exercise that involved deleting as many words as possible from a text without sacrificing the meaning, in order to improve readability. Sometimes, Writing=Scrapping.

Marese Jacobse – Schrijven is schrappen (original Dutch title)

DON'T RUSH IT

SLOW DOWN!

An experienced logistics consultant was often contracted as an advisor to fix issues in production chains. He told me he could often identify the problem after one walk through the factory but that if he gave his advice too soon, it would be rejected. His clients couldn't accept that a problem they had struggled with could be solved so quickly. So, what did he do? He went back to his office, continued with some other work, then presented his conclusion two weeks later. With a two-week delay built in, his advice would be accepted and implemented. Sometimes you can be **too swift** with your solution, even if it's the right one. Should you **slow down**?

SMALL, MEDIUM, LARGE

In the early days, McDonald's only offered a choice between Small and Large. A lot of customers chose Small, until they decided to make the Large a Medium and put an (abnormally sized) Large next to it. From that moment on, a majority of the customers chose the Medium option (formerly Large).

Always provide options for your clients to pick and choose from. If they are involved in the decision making, it becomes their choice. From now on, think options. Think McDonald's **Small, Medium, Large**.

PRE-WIRED FOR SUCCESS

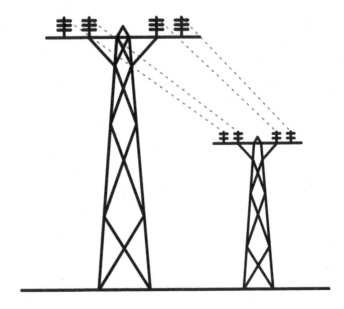

A good business presentation shouldn't contain anything the audience hasn't already seen before. **Pre-wire everything**. Walk all the relevant players through your findings before you gather them into a room. If you do this, you can be absolutely sure that your presentation will be a success and that the outcome will be the one you want. No surprises for the audience and none for you either.

Ethan M. Rasiel – *The McKinsey Way*

THE ONE-WORD PITCH

HOPE

According to Daniel Pink, in an era of short attention spans, you should be able to **pitch in a single word**. When someone says 'search' you think of Google. When someone says 'priceless', you might think of MasterCard. What's the one word that defines your brand? This applies to personal brand too, for example, the one word that defined President Barack Obama in 2008 was 'hope'. Reducing everything to one word is a great way to get focused and remove ambiguity.

Carmine Gallo – 'Six Simple And Irresistible Alternatives
To The Elevator Pitch'

TIMING IS EVERYTHING

Timing is everything in communication. Timing is in your control and it is a powerful tool. When you share your messages at the optimal date and time, they get the maximum impact. Everyone knows those organizations which send excessive emails resulting in mass unsubscribing. But timing is also important when communicating with employees or peers. And it's important to remember that timing is context related. Do you know the best moment to approach your boss to ask for a raise?

HOW DO YOU MAKE PEOPLE FEEL?

Maya Angelou, the famous American poet and author, made a wonderful comment on making an impact: 'People will forget what you said, people will forget what you did, but people will never forget how you made them feel.' It's not about what you say or do, it is **how you make someone feel** that gets you remembered. Keep that in mind. Listen to people. Be interested in them. There is no such thing as wasted kindness.

BANISH INCONSISTENCY

Nothing kills a report like **inconsistencies**. You know what it looks like. These reports where the numbers on one page differ from the numbers on the next. It's irritating and creates tedious, unnecessary discussions. It's almost better to be consistently wrong than inconsistent.

POWERFUL WRITING

There are eight rules on how to write a good story that people will enjoy reading. Powerful writing should:

1. be readable;
2. be focused;
3. develop gracefully;
4. flow;
5. be concrete;
6. be well suited to its audience;
7. be compelling and
8. be passionate.

Could you apply these rules to everything you write for your team? Could your team apply these rules to everything they write?

Lifehack.org – '8 qualities of powerful writing'

STAY ACTIVE

A lot of organizations write in the passive voice. It is often long-winded, indirect and avoids active verbs that show who actually did what, Writing in the passive voice causes tedium and ambiguity. When you **write in an active voice**, your sentences become a lot more readable. Use full stops and keep your sentences short.

Quinn, Faerman, Thompson and McGrath –
Becoming a Master Manager

A MASTERCLASS IN PRESENTING

1   2   3   4   5

If you want to create PowerPoint slides that won't put your audience to sleep, follow TED Coach Paul Jurczynski's 5 top tips for **presenting**:

1. Only include one idea per slide.
2. Have a consistent and thought-out colour scheme.
3. Don't go with the first visual that comes to mind.
4. Simple graphs are always best.
5. Don't be afraid of blank slides.

Paul Jurczynski, co-founder of Improve Presentation, Inc.com

WHY ARGUE IF YOU'RE WRONG

If you find yourself struggling to get your message across or unable to win people round to your position, take a step back. **It's no good arguing if you're in the wrong.** You won't need to when you're in the right.

EVERYONE JUDGES A BOOK BY ITS COVER

Apple doesn't have the best or the latest technology, but it presents its products perfectly in every possible detail. Packaging sells – **everyone judges a book by its cover**. So, spend some time on the layout of your next report. If it looks good, people are more likely to buy into it.

CREATE SCARCITY

You know how to get attention for something? Make it special. Make it **exclusive**. Make people want to be part of it. See what Apple does on every product launch. Availability is always limited. Apple **creates scarcity**, exploiting the gap between limited resources and limitless wants. How could you use scarcity to your advantage?

PART 9

EFFECTIVENESS

HEAD OFFICE

When asked whether he could remember his own phone number, Einstein answered: 'why should I memorize that, I never call myself'. This is a magnificent example of freeing up mental space, the approach David Allen advocates in *Getting Things Done*. Why try and remember everything? Just write stuff down and work with lists to **free up mental space, don't use your head as an office**. Avoid unnecessary mental baggage.

David Allen – *Getting Things Done*

INTUITION

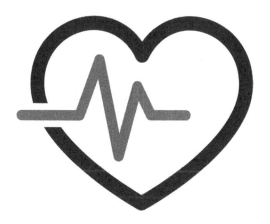

'Intuition is solidified experience,' a manager once said to me. Use it. Listen to it. Be careful when it tells you something's not right. It will probably come in the form of small clues you recognize from past experiences. Don't ignore them too easily.

DID YOU SPOT THE GORILLA?

Do you know the famous video clip of a gorilla walking around at a basketball game? You were told before watching the video to count how often the team passes the ball to one another and because you're so busy counting, **you miss the gorilla wandering around**. When you watch it again it's hard to believe how you missed it the first time. It's a good idea to remember this. Sometimes you need to zoom out to see the bigger picture.

Thanks to Alice de Graaf

ANGER MANAGEMENT 101

If something at work has made you so angry you want to go out there and kick some ass, just pause for a second to **manage your anger** before you end up making things worse. Try writing the story down from your perspective. Draft an email to the person you're angry at, but don't send it. Just getting it out of your system will calm you down. Sleep on it and then come back to your note. Was your reaction justified? Are you right to be upset about it? If so, you can still take action, but this time with a cooler head.

EAT THAT FROG

As Mark Twain once said, 'If it's your job to **eat a frog**, it's best to do it first thing in the morning.' The frog is the one thing on your to-do list that you have absolutely no motivation to do and that you're most likely to put off. But if you don't eat the frog, the frog will eat you. Once that one task is done, the rest of the day will be an easier ride. Eat it quick and you will get both momentum and a sense of accomplishment at the very start of your day.

HEARING WHAT ISN'T SAID

The most important thing in communication is **hearing what isn't said**. Non-verbal communication is often more important than what's actually said. Body language reveals a lot. So, after your next meeting, think back to how the participants handled themselves, what they said and didn't say and what messages passed between them through subtle, non-verbal cues. If you can read body language, your powers of communication will jump to an entirely new level.

IKIGAI

Stephen Covey's *7 Habits of Highly Effective People* is well known, but less famous is the book he wrote afterwards: *The 8th Habit*. This habit – Finding Your Voice – encourages introspection. Are you doing a job you feel passionate about? Are you making the best use of your talents? Does it match your values? And is there a need for it? At the intersection of these four dimensions, you will find your voice. In Japan, this is called **Ikigai** – 'a reason for being'. Have you found yours yet?

Stephen R. Covey – *The 8th Habit*

CHOOSE NOT TO BE BUSY

Busy is
... a choice
... reactivity
... a lack of focus
... distraction
... always on

Busyness is a choice and one that removes all other possibilities. Busy is reactive working, letting yourself be guided by others, letting yourself be guided by whatever comes your way instead of focusing on what really matters.

Busyness is working superficially, doing something because you have to, getting onto the treadmill without concentrating or focusing. Busy is being distracted by every email or notification you get. Being busy is always working, without taking a step back every now and then. **Have you chosen not to be busy?**

Tony Crabbe – *Busy*

YOUR EMAIL BANK ACCOUNT

Email is overwhelming. It's just not possible to handle the volume of emails most of us receive every day. So why not try this **email bank account** hack? You put a limit on the number of emails you send and commit to sending 10% less every 2 weeks. You now have a virtual 'budget' for emails. Before you hit 'send', ask yourself if you can afford this from your 'email balance'.

FIND YOUR ENERGY GAINS

Energy Gain

Energy Drain

Figuring out **what energizes you** and what saps your energy is an easy way to determine the kind of job you enjoy, the kind of work you like and what meetings to go to.

Funnily enough, energy has nothing to do with physical effort. Physical challenges often give you energy. Find where your energy gains come from and then concentrate on those things that build your energy and limit those that take it away.

INFORMATION OVERLOAD

9.11

When people complain about too much information, too many meetings, being busy or feeling overwhelmed, the problem is often something else entirely. It often comes down to the right priorities. Are you focusing on what really matters? **Information overload** is the result of a filter failure. If you are clear on your priorities, a lot of other stuff becomes much less relevant.

FOCUS ON WHAT YOU CAN CONTROL

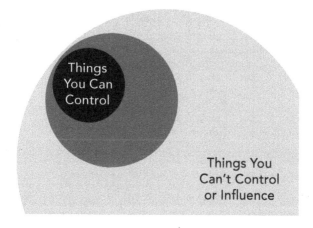

Things You Can Control

Things You Can't Control or Influence

You should **only ever worry about things you can control** or influence.

Many people get unnecessarily preoccupied with things outside their area of control, which only causes frustration and stress. If you can't control it, let it go. You don't have to just accept it, of course. You can also try to bring things into your area of control. But until that happens, it's out of your hands.

A QUICK EMAIL HACK

Here's another **email inbox management** hack. I have a single folder for each workday. And in addition, a folder labelled 'waiting' and a folder labelled 'completed'. A few times a day I check my inbox and determine what to do with an email. If I can do it in 5 minutes, I'll do it right away. Everything else I assign to the day of the week that it has to be done by and deal with it then. Items that are due after the current week are placed in 'Friday' and are re-assigned the following week. This way you maintain a clear overview and deal with everything in the right priority order.

BOUNDED RATIONALITY

As a manager, you don't make decisions as rationally as you might think. In an ideal situation you have a clear view of all available options and the possible consequences which makes it easy to choose the best option. But this is not how it actually works.

You never really have all the options, you never know exactly what the consequences are, which means that you won't find the best solution, but you might find an acceptable outcome. It's comforting that there is a theory behind this: **Bounded Rationality** explains that you can only do the best you can do, so you shouldn't feel bad if the outcome isn't the best.

THINK THE OPPOSITE

9.15

WHATEVER
YOU THINK

EHT KNIHT
ETISOPPO

Changing your thinking can have powerful results, so try the Paul Arden trick of **thinking the opposite**. When it was my daughter's bedtime, she did everything she could to postpone it as long as possible until I turned it into a game: 'Who can get upstairs first?' It also applies to organizational issues.

Sometimes saying you don't want something – like a position or a role – makes you get it. And vice versa.

Paul Arden – *Whatever You Think, Think the Opposite*

KNOW THE RATIOS

Have you noticed how some people seem to have an almost supernatural ability to instantly pinpoint the strengths and weaknesses of an annual plan, budget or commercial proposal? What's the secret? **Knowing the ratios.** Knowing your organization's key ratios means you can quickly check a plan for its soundness. Do you have them at your fingertips?

KEEP A POSITIVE MINDSET

If you do your work with a **positive mindset**, beautiful things happen. Positive energy is contagious – it stimulates creativity and curiosity. It works the other way round too. If you become a complainer, your problems swell and deplete your energy levels. When you decide not to complain, a lot of positive energy is released. Give it a try. Whistle to work and whistle on the job. Soon everyone will be doing it.

THE ONE THING

There are always a million things on your plate. Endless to-do lists, a ton of tasks and even more priorities. But there is always one thing that should require your attention above all else. **One thing** that will really make a difference. One thing that, if done well, will have an extraordinary impact on you and your business.

So ask yourself the question every now and again: 'What is the One Thing for me right now?'

Keller & Papasan – *The One Thing*

IDLENESS

Idleness is especially wonderful after a period of productivity and you are more productive after a period of relaxation. It's all about balance.

Everyone is different, everyone has their own rhythm. You have to take that rhythm into account when planning your daily routine. You'll function better if you can control the rhythm. Do you have the freedom and flexibility to do that? Do you give your team that freedom?

THE CAMPFIRE QUESTION

Life goes on with all its ups and downs regardless of anything you might do, but that's no reason to take a back seat. If you're not paying attention, other people and things will quietly take control of your life, whether it's the demands of your boss or clients, family responsibilities or social engagements. Every once in a while, ask yourself the **campfire question**: 'Where am I in this story?' You might find it's time to change course.

Onno Aerden – *De kampvuurvraag* (original Dutch title)

ABOUT THE AUTHOR

Dr Roel de Graaf (MBA, MBI) is a seasoned entrepreneur, consultant, and author with over 35 years of experience in business working with managers and executives.

Throughout his career, Roel has been committed to helping businesses achieve their full potential. His passion for entrepreneurship, innovation, and process improvement has made him a trusted advisor and partner for businesses seeking to optimize their operations, leverage technology, and drive growth.

Additionally, Roel is a lecturer at Nyenrode Business University in the Advanced IT Program. He is frequently invited to share his knowledge at conferences on topics such as Change, IT Strategy, and Governance.

His interventions are always aimed at connecting people involved to collaborate towards a common goal. Roel's philosophy is that it should seem natural and intuitive for everyone involved. When this is achieved, change will happen (effortlessly).

AHACKADAY — THE BUSINESS HACK APP

After enjoying the business hacks in this book, are you looking for more inspiration? Consider purchasing the accompanying app 'Ahackaday' that is available for the iPhone. The Ahackaday app gives you a business hack for every day of the year. The widget on your home screen is a great way to start your day!

365 hacks — a hack for every day of the year.

The hacks are organized into themed sections according to months where that theme is most likely high on your agenda. The themes can also be viewed via a menu so that you can find them quickly if you need them. Most enjoyable however, is simply flipping through the hacks. You can use the randomizer to be surprised by a random hack and to see how it applies to your daily routine.

(The app is not free. This is for a reason: 'If something is free, then you are the product.' This app does not collect data from you and does not contain advertisements.)

https://apps.apple.com/us/app/ahackaday/id1610770740

Alternatively, you can find this app in the Apple App Store by searching 'Ahackaday' or 'Roel de Graaf'.

This app is produced solely by the author. The Publisher assumes no responsibility for this app.

Would you like your people to read this book?

If you would like to discuss how you could bring these ideas to your team, we would love to hear from you. Our titles are available at competitive discounts when purchased in bulk across both physical and digital formats. We can offer bespoke editions featuring corporate logos, customized covers, or letters from company directors in the front matter can also be created in line with your special requirements.

We work closely with leading experts and organizations to bring forward-thinking ideas to a global audience. Our books are designed to help you be more successful in work and life.

For further information, or to request a catalogue, please contact: **business@johnmurrays.co.uk**

John Murray Business is an imprint of John Murray Press.